Hit it!

2

Nat and Meg

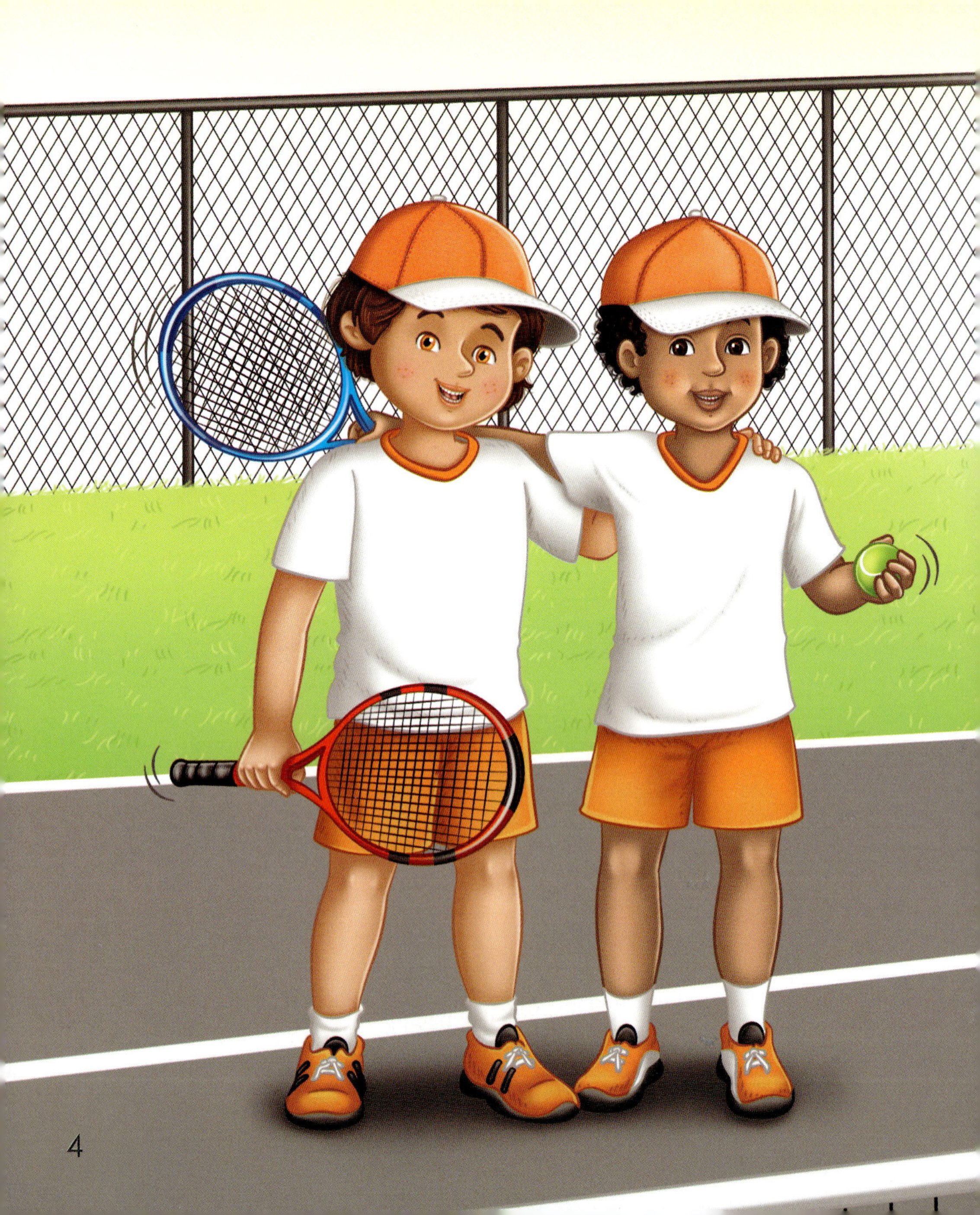

Dan and Tim

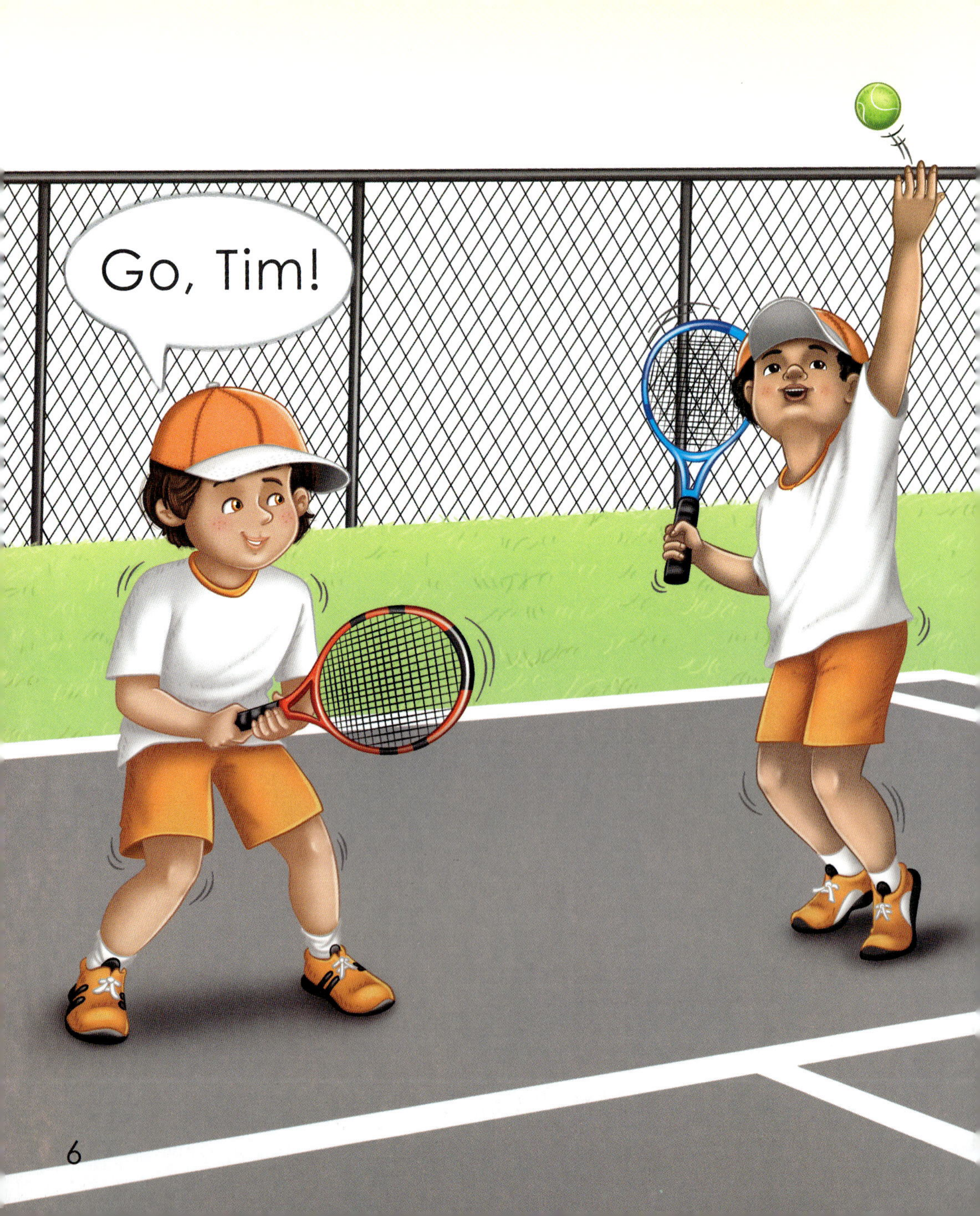
Go, Tim!

Tim has a big hit.

8

It hits the net.

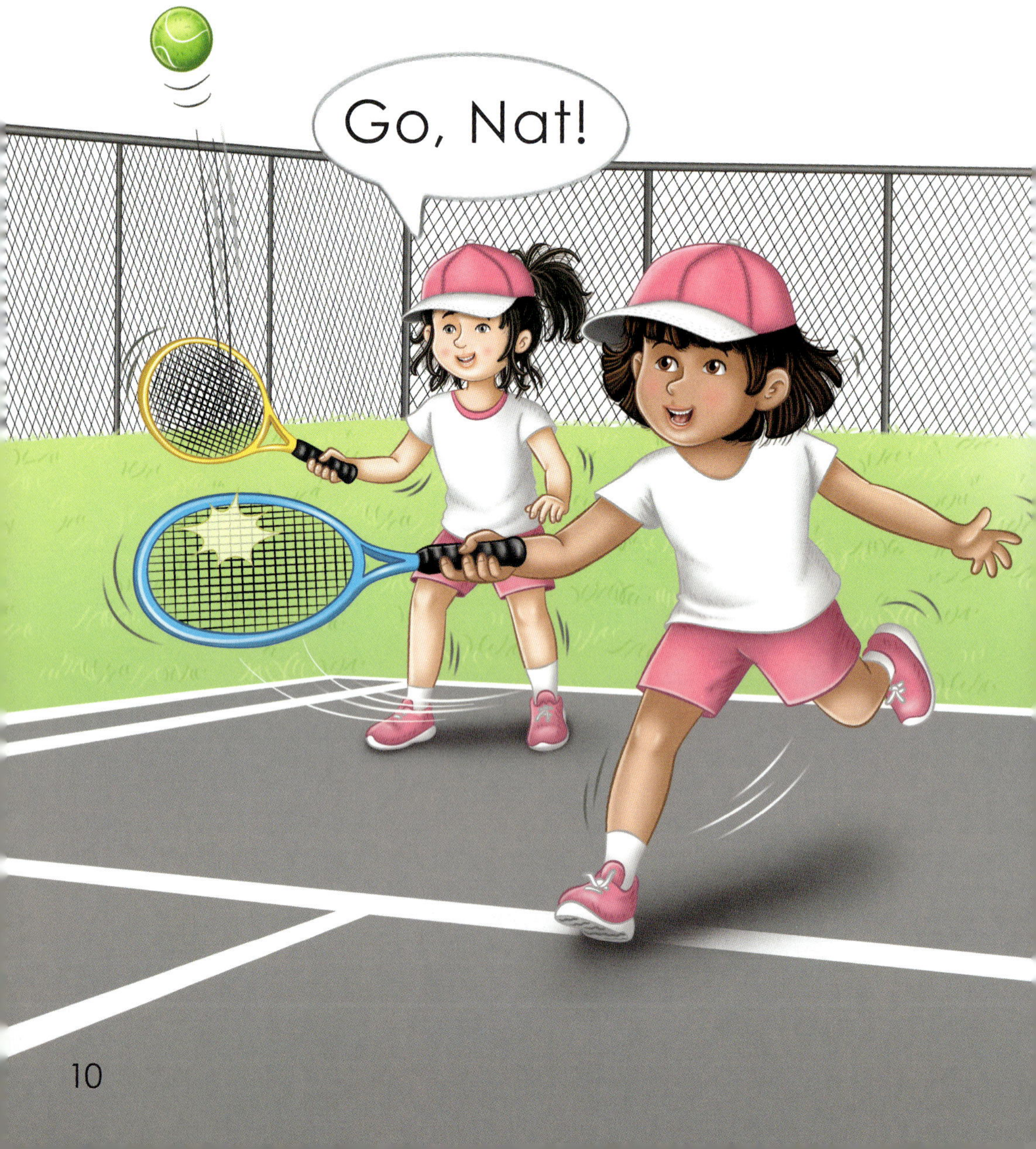
Go, Nat!

Nat hits it up.
Up, up, up.

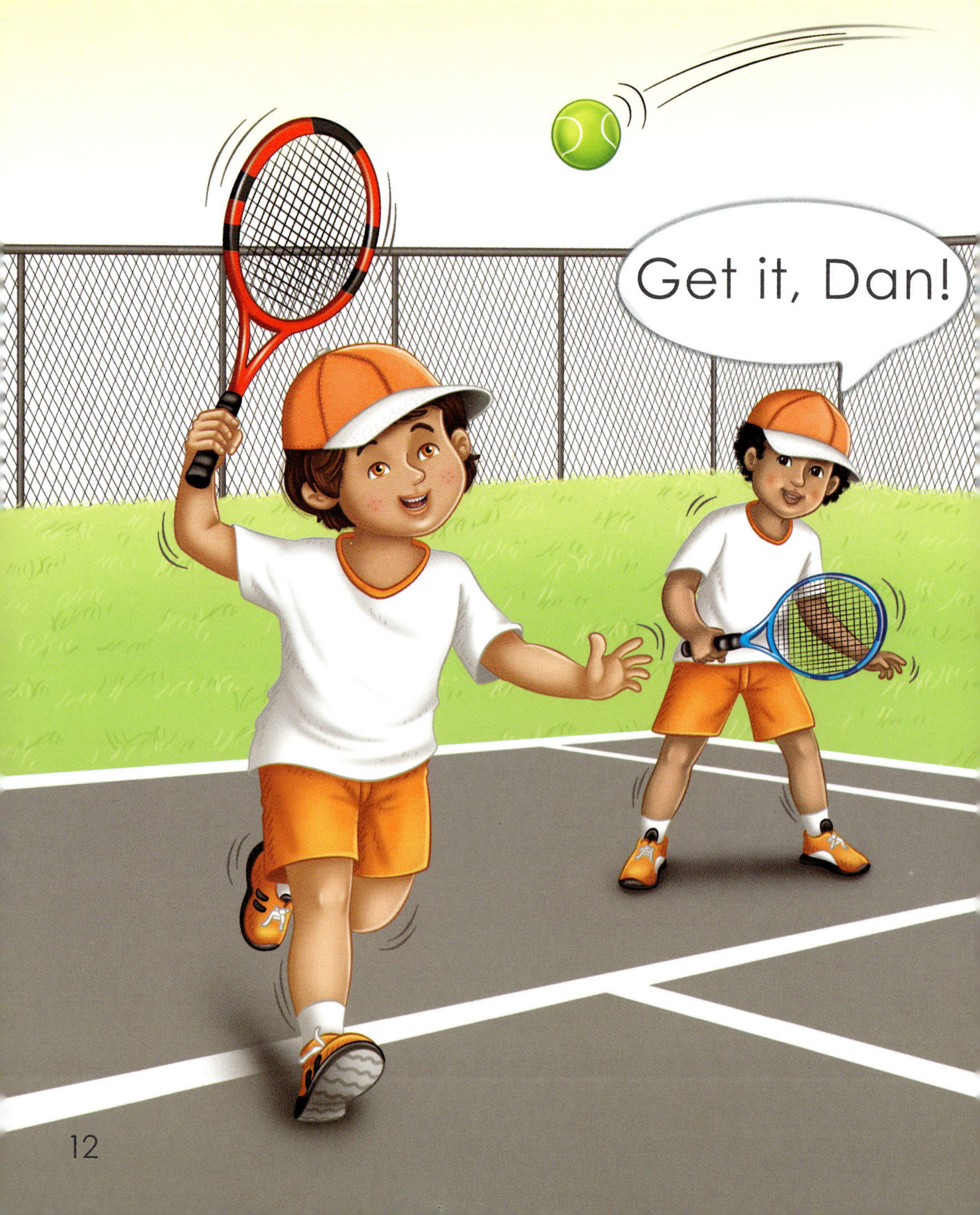
Get it, Dan!

Dan runs to it.

14

Pam gets it,
not Dan.

Hit it! Level 2, Set 2: Story 12

Before reading

Say the sounds: g o b h e r f u l

Practise blending the sounds: Nat Meg Dan Tim big hit hits net up get runs Pam gets not

High-frequency words: it a **Tricky words:** and go has the to
Vocabulary check: net – a tennis net stretches across the court and you have to hit the ball over it

Story discussion: What game are the children playing in this story? Have you ever played tennis?

Teaching points: Check that children can say the phonemes /g/ /o/ /b/ /h/ /e/ /r/ /u/, and that they can identify the grapheme that goes with each phoneme.
Check that they can read sentences ending in exclamation marks with appropriate expression.
Check that children can identify and read the tricky words: and, go, has, the, to.

After reading

Comprehension:
- What game are the children playing?
- Who gives the ball a big hit?
- What happens to the ball when Nat hits it?
- What would you say to Pam, if you were one of the children in the story?

Fluency: Speed-read the words again from the inside front cover.